ONCE UPON a ON POLISHED DYSTOPIA

ONCE UPON A POLISHED DYSTOPIA

*Outré Humor Tales
and a One-Act Comedy Play*

BY
RORRY NIGHTTRAIN EAST

ACKNOWLEDGEMENTS

For Dr. Robert Stuckey

A long story shortened – this author
started his first book with a borrowed
pencil from one of Pastor Stuckey's pews.
Much obliged for that, sir. Also put a
bit of something into the offering plate
toward the posterity of other
writer visitors.

◈

PREFACE

Crowned-dreams drip,
thoughts soak and settle;
see God upon someone's face:
It is in an old, worn house
that no longer matches
their golden soul.

Rorry Nighttrain East
Silver City, New Mexico
June 31, 2015

TaBLE OF CONTENTS

PASTOR SKYCANDY'S GOSPEL

THE RiGoR MORTiS REViVAL HOUR

Most of the kind folks around old east San Jose, California call me "Janitor Moses." But I want to tell ya about a run-down, wooden church, back in the 1950s, just off of Story Road, called "Flippant Temple." You heard me right; it was called "Flippant Temple" because the late Sadie Flippant gave her empty church building to that no-good and crooked Sugar B. Skycandy, and she had it put in her will that I'd be the permanent building and grounds keeper—paid, of course.

Sugar B. Skycandy was so crooked that he went out and bought a $19.95 theology certificate and promptly opened up shop. And I'm surprised that "Pastor Skycandy" didn't put superglue on the wooden pews just to keep people there. He began with all his phony sewer sermons. Why, he was even telling people they could get rich and famous just by going to Flippant Temple and crossin' their fingers on the full moon at his drive-thru church window.

Uh-huh, those were some hurtin' days, and when he tried to open a "Soul-Food Bank" I darn near did "The Funky Chicken" down the aisles with my arm winding backwards like a broken clock. I'm a stoic guy, too.

Then it went from bad to worse when Pastor Skycandy was forced to hire on several of his former conmen friends as a favor; Flippant Temple ended up with people like Deacon Dubious and Elder Younger (a thirteen year old boy) and Secretary Megaphone (Miss Tell-All).

That's not even the worst of it. It was about that time when "Stroll" and "Baby-Doll" began sanctuary hopping from "Our Lady of the Boulevard Church" and they took over Pastor Skycandy's Singles Group. I'm tellin' ya — Pastor Skycandy had become the High Priest of Stupidity on steroids without any church-y/church fandango in his vocabulary.

Even the choir director wore earmuffs, and he carried tunes around in a bucket full of cobwebs, because he had two tin ears from a war accident that he couldn't admit.

But probably the funniest thing I ever saw was how Pastor Skycandy had visited other churches out of town to learn his Christian-eese, and he had gotten it all wrong. I'm tellin' ya, the man was Hope's Poverty — on an exponential leap backwards by itself. I mean . . . He was teachin' people how to "Gallows Gossip," how to "Back-Bite To the Bone," and how to "Be a Great Stumbling Block" to all others. He'd learned all the wrong things.

Yep, Pastor Skycandy's spiritual cyanide was so bad that folks came from miles around just to learn "the Pride of Man" from Mr. Backwards himself. He was even sellin' holy water from the toilet bowl backs that he ripped-off from monastery restrooms.

I was gettin' ready to make like the Red Sea and part the day that Skycandy found out his Maker wasn't named See's Candy.

"Tell me . . . Janitor Moses," Pastor Skycandy said, "is it true that the Accuser does his best work behind stained glass?"

"You ought to know," I replied. "You'd need a time machine if you wanted folks to backslide any more than they have . . ."

Pastor Skcandy half-moaned the words out, "Maybe I could give a sermon on Bible Bingo!"

"Nobody throws 'the Good Book' open and points to a passage like a Bingo game anymore." I laughed. "Just start tellin' the truth."

After poor Skycandy started tellin' the truth, his church shrank from three Sunday services and hundreds of folks lookin' to get rich and famous down to only twelve people.

The positive flipside is, we founded an honest ministry college with only a few people and changed our corner of the world with less talk and more practical kindness. What's the moral of my story here?

Hope marinated in Skycandy
often makes a flippant meal
for most bellyachers.

LONESOME ARE THE STUPID SLEUTHS

BULLET NOTE:

Not since the first printing press was invented in 1450 has there been such an adored, and yet completely inept, gumshoe detective who's gone on a joyride in a coma, while delving into the vagaries of femme fatales and lawbreakers. Yes, "Jack Hammer," in all his clueless demeanor, continues to pound the cold, night streets from his supreme bedroom home office (at his aged-mother's house in Bakersfield), and with a strange world acclaim.

Some people are even saying that our favorite above sleuth still holds the Guinness Book record on "The Private Eye's" ingrown ego, about his own charm with women, which has outgrown all human laughter itself.

MS. APOCALYPSE DAWN

She walked into the room and her hips swiveled; they almost waved me back down the road. Then Jean DeFormed said, "I've got a second-rate job for a fifth-rate Private Eye. You want it?"

"Let's skip the paperwork," Jack Hammer exclaimed. "I'll take it."

Jean DeFormed said, "My husband is a medical doctor, and I think he's a quack."

"Why do you think he's a quack?" Jack asked.

"Well," Jean DeFormed softly admitted, "whenever his patients go to leave his office — instead of shaking hands — he hands them his *bill!*"

"I see what you mean." Jack Hammer sighed. "But I can't take your case right now, because I have woman troubles."

Apocalypse Dawn said, "Is it anything you wish to get off your chest?"

"Yes." Jack Hammer moaned. "Her name is 'Explosive Joy,' and you can bet your Rockford's trailer on the beach — she wants her five dollars back that she lent me for my mail-order Private Eye courses . . ."

"Maybe you should be in another type of business," Apocalypse Dawn suggested, "because you don't seem to have a clue."

"Yeah, lonesome are the stupid sleuths," he cried. "I'm so old that I came out to California on a wagon train, and I used to even teach horses how to talk — it was at a job called 'Pony Express!' It's no wonder I'm a washout with the ladies."

"Well," she suggested again, "why don't you start by no longer picking up women with sinister names like: Dirty Diane, Filthy Fay, Sniper Sally, Mass-Destruction Milly, Marilyn Manhunter, Easily Dunn, Big Bore Barbara, Nuclear Nadine, Roberta Redrum — and who knows what else to expect."

"Okay," Jack Hammer said, "I'm going to have a divorce party from all of 'em. Maybe I'll even fake my death again."

Apocalypse Dawn said, "That didn't work the first two times you tried it."

"Yeah, but this time . . ." he said, "my eulogy will go into great detail about how I hated *mayonnaise* . . . and people will weep for miles around over the fact I actually thought of *mayo* as liquid-Hitler. Then they will finally know that Mayo was-and-is a culinary crime and the meal-bomb that killed me. You can even tell them I'm shaking hands with Elvis up in that big condiment kitchen in the sky. 'Thank-you very much . . .'"

But what do I know? I'm just your basic

clue-antagonist—I'm not really what you'd call "presidential material." But I do know . . . that meeting—a horde of fascists—as an overnight guest means you've probably just slept in the "Lincoln bedroom."

◆

Reality fought
nuts/bolts/warts and all,
yet the earth may
still have a
screw loose.

◆

◆

Sugar-coated
failure
is mediocrity
on steroids.

◆

STUPIDITY AND THE COLD NIGHT STREETS

Yeah, lonesome are the stupid sleuths. I sure felt like a plain-clothes nudist without a dental plan for machine gun pie. Whatever that means. But I bit the bullet anyway . . .

Now this might sound kinda like a 'Deja Moo' (that's the feeling you've heard all this same BULL before), yet I got tired of always being an indigent Private Eye. Why, I probably tried almost every dumb job in the world. I'm *so* old that I played my first game of "Poker" with a stick and a dinosaur!

Thus, I decided to go deep undercover as a brand new Monk/Detective. I'm even thinking of selling my Rockford's trailer on the beach and pretending I'm a wandering Monk who's taste-tested too much of his own wine. I'll still be a real Private Eye, of course (wink, wink). Whenever people ask me what I'm doing, I'll just say, "Remember now . . . to be 'clueless' means to be blindsided by the true emptiness of your own foresight's photographic memory — that you've already forgotten to buy film for." Yeah; stupidity and the cold night streets don't really mix well, but they do make a super nice recipe for tossed-brain salad dressing.

So I took my very next caper from a prim and lacy librarian gal who just happened to be a horseracing bookie (on the side), and then I caught her attention by saying, "Hay"; I mean ... "Hey!"

THAT'S THE WAY THE LIBRARIAN BOUNCES

Sure, sure . . . I'm with the "Junior Varsity" of the so-called Depraved—because first I solve the crime, then I haven't got a clue as to why burning a used copy of *Leaves of Grass* was called "Poetry-cide" in the first place!

That's just the way the Librarian always bounces . . .

I was lookin' for a stolen, first edition copy of Mad Magazine, and the first place I thought of to look was at the city dump.

Some people say I'm a nitwit—but that's just because I work without a net. And the reason I don't have any cents . . . is . . . that's just the high price of "Low-Living." It also seems that in not finding that Mad Magazine at the city dump (because it was already in the Smithsonian Institute), I felt like having a funeral for a clue; such things reminded me that even though I can't have that Magazine, I still mourn Rodney Dangerfield's death. I often think about how he said, "When I was born I was so ugly the doctor slapped my mother." He also said, "I came from a stupid family during 'The Civil War.' My great uncle fought for the west." It's only then, that I really wonder if Rodney and I aren't somehow related?

ALL COMEUPPANCE IS BENEATH MY AXE

DUMB . . . DA, DUMB, DUMB . . . ! DUMB . . . DA, DUMB, DUMB DUUUUMMMB!

Yes, you might think that I'm about as fake as a Beverly Hills, Salvation Army, gold rubber band, money clip—but crime is still my meal ticket. This may even sound like a requiem for a Gumshoe, but I've got lousy taste in lady stumbling blocks.

So there I was . . . in love again . . . and it was with another trailer-park princess. Her name was Deathbed Debbie. You can bet your Rockford's trailer on the beach that she was an ultra-high-maintenance babe, too.

Although, first—did I ever tell you that my uncle was in the Navy? Yeah; he was on a submarine sponsored by the Cubs Baseball Team. Yep, they even had their name and a picture of a baseball mitt on the side of their sub. But it never won any battles because the ship was called . . . the "Sub Mitt!" Anyway, that same uncle ran away with Deathbed Debbie the first week I met her. Now I know where they got the word UFO: Uh-huh, because Deathbed Debbie and my old, girlfriend-stealing uncle just had a baby together. Yes . . . a UFO is really just an "Unfortunate Father's Obsticle," as Debbie always throws flying cups and saucers at him. I really think that *stupidity* must be a natural aphrodisiac, because if you're stupid enough you are really gonna get screwed by Jezabel herself on the frozen altar of dead-works.

Just call me the hatchet man, 'cause I got back at my uncle, but good — and all comeuppance is beneath my axe.

So . . . what's the point of my self-absorbed and sinister little detective tale here? It's reminder that if you wanna be a big wheel P.I., be sure to watch more *Ironside* reruns on your petty-dictator box. (That's a TV.)

The upshot is this: If you seriously want to have some formidable street-cred with all those sweet ladies out there, just keep your wallet open and your zipper closed. And another thing: You might even think about lowering your standards to the point that even a "trailer park princess" looks like Buckingham Palace material. It couldn't hoit!

BARRACUDA TALE

BARRACUDA TALE

"A One-Act Comedy"
PLAY

BY
RORRY NIGHTTRAIN EAST

INTRODUCTION

One thing that I've always liked about great thinkers is that no one is ever wrong in philosophy. You can be completely wrong and theoretically still be completely right.

May I now pose one profound and socially-redeeming question? Okay, then . . . "What is WHAT? And where is WHEN!" Is it all becoming so very clear now? Not to Platonize you too much, because Plato's Greek to me, but you are never wrong in philosophy. But above all— have love.

Cast of Characters:

CAPTAIN U.C. BOTTOM

The main character—who is a boat owner—and also has a distressful, recurring nightmare about a barracuda. He is unaware that he is actually aquaphobic—because so many of his ships have sunk. He's being treated at the "Inn Security," which used to be called the "Security Inn" before a mild hurricane blew its sign down and then "Sandbag" (a lazy handyman) put the sign back again, only backwards. Doctor Indiahouse is the captain's in-house vacationing psychiatrist. (He's treating the captain for bad dreams.)

SANDBAG

He dresses like a bearded transient. He's the inept, resort-motel's handyman. He's a frustrated musician, and he carries a guitar with him everywhere.

FLOATER

He spends all his time on a red raft in the Gulf. He's usually visible from a distance, but has No Lines. He is the symbol of what a truevacation is all about: rest!

DOCTOR INDIAHOUSE

(Accent from India.) A funny and overly-syrupy psychiatrist who wears three-piece suits on the beach.

ZILLA GREEN

(As in "xylo"-phone.) A motel guest and perhaps the only truly normal person in the group, who is curious about the Barracuda Tale.

REELY OLFF

(Last name sounded: "off.") The proprietor and perpetuator of the "Inn Security" on the beach who is "really off" in a humorous way.

BIRD NORTH

A general friend and sunbather as well as a motel guest who is a snow-bird down from Michigan.

EXTRAS

Bonfire scene and barracuda running up the end-seating aisles.

SeTTiNG:

TIME

In the mid-spring at the height of the southwest Florida's vacation season, 2004.

PLACE

This comedy takes place at the Security Inn resort-motel on Fort Myers Beach, Florida.

Act 1

THE CURTAIN RISES. We see a low-key, re-sort-motel, check-in desk, and the surrounding chairs of the television lounge. It is entered from the front door at the left. The main lobby contains a view of the ocean's horizon through wide open French doors. Outdoors to right stage:

CAPTAIN U.C. BOTTOM is having a stressful, recurring nightmare about an aggressive barracuda that once sought him when one of his ships previously sank.

A parrot is squawking in the background.

>   CAPTAIN U.C. BOTTOM
>   (the captain speaks aloud, to his
>   imaginary parrot)
> Inasmuch as I *love* marine-architecture, you could say we are all architects of our own future. And perhaps a Barracuda Tale wouldn't be swimming against current tastes — What's that? I know you're an imaginary parrot! Huh? Yes. What an awful dream. The resort's visiting doctor assures me that it's nothing more than a biting
>   (MORE)

BARRACUDA TALE

CAPTAIN U.C. BOTTOM (cont'd)
sense of insecurity—at a depth that I
haven't gotten in touch with yet.

The parrot gives a stupid SQUAWK.

DOCTOR INDIAHOUSE
(walks up and speaks to the
imaginary parrot as well)
Pardon me, animal enthusiasts. Inter-
preting nightmares can be difficult.
These things can take years discover.

CAPTAIN U.C. BOTTOM
Yes. Though each night when I sleep,
those pinnacles of undersea canyon
come rushing back to me:

*That same man in the swimming mask
is still wading beneath the waters there,
and he's facing a sharp-nosed barracuda.
The sturdy man then always fights to rise
to the surface as quickly as possible. The
fierce fish faces him—only a yard away.
Nose to nose-mask—all the way up to the
surface—they go together! Finally, the ex-
cited man climbs aboard the stern-steps of
an opulent cruising vessel, and he makes
his way up to a flying bridge. Then this
man pulls a pair of binoculars to his sun-
burned face, and then . . . I awake! It's me!*
(MORE)

CAPTAIN U.C. BOTTOM (cont'd)
The next thing I know . . .I'm safely in
my own cottage at the Security Inn,
on the peaceful shores of Fort Myers
Beach—and all is well. So . . . I think
I'll stay at this Inn . . .

The parrot's funny SQUAWK, again.

DOCTOR INDIAHOUSE
Yes, you've been making great prog-
ress. But let's try and get rid of the—
fake parrot. It's just a security blanket,
you know.

CAPTAIN U.C. BOTTOM and DOCTOR INDI-
AHOUSE freeze.

ZILLA GREEN walks in to the front office,
where REELY OLFF'S back is turned toward
her, and REELY is sorting postcards. Each time
ZILLA—whose name is sounded like "xylophone"—walks in, zippy notes of a xylophone
play.

ZILLA GREEN
Ms. Olff? Did you know that your sign
out front reads backwards? Instead of
the "Security Inn", it reads . . . the "Inn
Security!"

REELY OLFF
(snotty-attitude)
Young woman. Most of our guests are so forward-thinking that it corrects the sign's problem. Besides! It gives a terrific fizz to the atmosphere here. Take Captain U.C. Bottom, for instance . . ."

ZILLA GREEN
(rolls her eyes)
No. You take him.

She turns and leaves the insanely-older woman behind.

ZILLA walks through the open patio doors to where a lazy handyman, SANDBAG, is lounging away without a care in the world. Thus, intrigued, she stops beside his lounge chair.

ZILLA GREEN
(laughs at his audacity)
Mister . . . Sandbag? Industrious general-handyman, I presume?

SANDBAG
(in a garbled, mumbled voice)
Yeah, man? I mean . . . woman. Now that you've been livin' here on the beach for a month, tell me what you think of the Florida way?

ZILLA GREEN
I'd say . . . the Gulf of Mexico has been
a good influence. Why do you ask?

SANDBAG
No real reason. But if you knew whole
story about the barracudas, then that
would be a true accomplishment!

ZILLA GREEN
(riddled)
What? . . . Barracudas?

SANDBAG
(suddenly distracted)
Look Zilla! Over there! It's Bird North.
(he scratches his leather-like
skin and mangy beard)
She's walking on the shore. How
would you like to meet a real snow-
bird sometime?

ZILLA GREEN
Sure. But you know you put our motel
sign up backwards — don't you?

SANDBAG
You-bet-your Dry Tortugas! One bird
on the shoreline is worth two . . . in the
palm.

ZILLA GREEN
(scratches her head)
Uh . . . what did you just say?

SANDBAG
It means: The right woman from any
distance is the right woman for me.

ZILLA GREEN
Oh. I thought that's what you said.
And it still makes no sense

ZILLA now walks back indoors to meet up with
REELY OLFF.

REELY OLFF is talking to the *imaginary parrot* at
the front desk.

REELY OLFF
Polly want a bologna sandwich?

BARRACUDA TALE

ZILLA GREEN
(strolls up to the desk pleasantly)
This place must be crazy! Sandbag won't take responsibility for putting the motel sign up backwards.

Just then, a gauche-sounding xylophone plays in the background every time the name 'Zilla' is mentioned.

REELY OLFF
Oh, you again? You know, you can call me "Reely" if you want to. Because I understand that your name, "Zilla," is like the prefix of a musical instrument of graduating lengths that is hit with small hammers.

ZILLA GREEN
(frustrated)
I can think of somebody who needs to be hit with a hammer! Doesn't anyone seek a sense of reality here?

REELY OLFF
(indignant)
Wait right there. Don't you talk to my parrot that way!

The invisible parrot SQUAWKS!

ZILLA GREEN
(realizes she's in a pseudo nut-
house)
Yes . . . I mean . . . no. I was really off!

REELY OLFF
(feeds the nonexistent parrot a
cracker)
Excuse me. Excuse me! But I'm the
only one around here that's Reely Olff!

Parrot: "ARK, ARK, Polly want a cracker."

ZILLA GREEN
You'd be surprised!!!

REELY OLFF
Shhhh . . . the parrot is sleeping.

Parrot: "Nighty, night."

ZILLA GREEN
(pities the proprietor now)
Say . . . you look a little down in the
mouth, Reely. Why don't we have a
big bonfire on the beach tonight?

REELY OLFF
Yeah. Maybe we'll see some "real"
barracudas, too!

As the light goes off . . .

BARRACUDA TALE

The two gals walk off. They join the party on the opposite stage.

As Tiki lights come on, a barbecue on the beach and a party begins. All the actors join in by bringing their own folding lawn chairs.

An outdoor patio is decked-out with colored Tiki lamps. Sounds of crickets in background, with reflections of light off water.

> REELY OLFF
> (to her party guests)
> Attention everyone! . . . Attention! I'm so glad you could join us here, on this evening, on the festive occasion. While it might be true that most of you Florida residents are of a more mature nature, nevertheless . . . the night is young! Even though you're a crowd that's crowding fifty!
>
> All kidding aside. Doctor Indiahouse, do you have any comments to make about our perpetually-youthful group here tonight?!

> DOCTOR INDIAHOUSE
> (only person in a 3-piece suit, with an accent from India)
> Madam Olff, thank you for letting me
> (MORE)

DOCTOR INDIAHOUSE (cont'd)
check-in with the group. I just want to
share 'n' care, and care-n-share.

As they say in my old country: When
the Great Cobra makes his abode in the
night sands . . . *use a cement beach towel!*

REELY OLFF
You're welcome, I think. Now, is there
anyone else who would like to speak
before the party begins?

CAPTAIN U.C. BOTTOM
(in a funny pirate voice)
Aye Madam, I would like to speak
about the barracuda! With great teeth,
the size of . . .

DOCTOR INDIAHOUSE
(stands and interrupts)
But you're getting over your bad
dreams, Captain!

CAPTAIN U.C. BOTTOM
Aye. How the mighty have fallen . . .
or . . . sunken to the bottom of the sea
in this case.

DOCTOR INDIAHOUSE
You can rise above it, Captain!

BARRACUDA TALE

CAPTAIN U.C. BOTTOM
(climbs into his own comical
anti-wisdom)
Aye. Aye. These are high times. Right,
me hearty parrot?

The Parrot now gives a silly SQUAWK!

REELY OLFF
(takes command)
Uh . . . how fascinating, Captain. And
now, let's light the bonfire and let the
party begin!

DOCTOR INDIAHOUSE
(on the spur of the moment as
the crowd disperses to dance or
talk)
Uh, Zilla . . . I'd like you to meet Bird
North.

ZILLA GREEN
Oh, hi! I saw you walking on the beach
earlier today. You seemed so content.
I didn't have the heart to bother you.

BIRD NORTH
(bizarre blonde beauty)
Nice to meet ya . . . Zilla, I really do
exist—unlike a few certain "parrots"
around here.

Rorry NightTrain East

A funny background parrot SQUAWK!

DOCTOR INDIAHOUSE
(interrupts with a feather-brained discourse)

Light music and dancing in background.

DOCTOR INDIAHOUSE (cont'd)
Pardon me, ladies, but I may just have some rather weighty and urgent information that could help you cope better here at the illustrious "Inn Security."

BIRD NORTH
(uncomfortable silence)

ZILLA GREEN
(puzzled look with an open jaw)
Daylight is slowly dawning.

DOCTOR INDIAHOUSE
When you're feeling the effects of being "really off," always remember it could be a compliment. Because there's an old fable about a man who was once committed to an insane asylum, holding his fingers onto a fence and just looking outward. Then another man drove by him and had a flat tire, right there, in front of his peering eyes
(MORE)

BARRACUDA TALE

DOCTOR INDIAHOUSE (cont'd)
and grip upon the fence. So the man
on the outside, who had the flat, began
to take the newly-punctured tire off of
the car. And while doing so, he acci-
dently kicked the "lug nuts" through a
grate and down inside a drainage hole.

BIRD NORTH
(perplexed)
Uh . . . lug nuts?

ZILLA GREEN
(like a powder-puff mechanic)
There are five lug nuts on each wheel and they hold the tires on, my snow-Bird friend!

DOCTOR INDIAHOUSE
(continues)
As I was saying. The man behind the fence of the insane asylum said, "Why don't you go around to the other wheels and take one lug nut off of each of them, then put the spare tire on with the extra-borrowed lug nuts?" The driver said, *"Hey! You're pretty smart. Why are you living in an asylum, anyway?"* The man holding onto the fence replied, *"I might be crazy?! But I'm not stupid!"*

BIRD NORTH, with a wide-eyed grin, turns her wrist upside down, and, with her elbow facing outward, she puts her hand between her teeth and shakes the hand back and forth.

ZILLA GREEN
Say, I've heard a lot of nutty things
(MORE)

ZILLA GREEN (cont'd)
around here. But why is everyone around these parts obsessed with barracudas?

BIRD NORTH
Guess you haven't heard about Captain U.C. Bottom's dream? Or . . . have you?

ZILLA GREEN
(fidgets nervously)
Uh . . . *No*. Not Exactly?

BIRD NORTH
Don't worry, Zilla, you will. This place is kind of an insane asylum in disguise as a resort motel.

ZILLA GREEN
Huh? Bird, now you're starting to sound like Doctor Indiahouse.

BIRD NORTH
Yeah?! Think about it for a minute. We've got Doctor Indiahouse, an in-house psychiatrist, who's treating Captain U.C. Bottom, who is having bad, recurring barracuda dreams! We have Reely Olff, the proprietor — who is "really off," if you know what I
(MORE)

BIRD NORTH (cont'd)
mean. Then we've got Floater . . . the man who represents the quintessential vacationer, as he just lies around on a red raft out in the Gulf all day . . .

ZILLA GREEN
True. I guess you could say it's all a kind of a nut house at the water's edge.

BIRD NORTH
(laughing at the idea in a com-ic-tone)
Yeah. We've also got an *imaginary parrot* and a *lazy handyman named Sandbag.*

A silly background parrot SQUAWK!

ZILLA GREEN
So, what could be worse?

BIRD NORTH
Worst of all . . . This resort motel used to be called the Security Inn. But now its omnipresent sign has been put up backwards. And it now reads . . . Inn Security! While U.C. Bottom continually rattles our cages with his stupid barracuda dreams. None of us will rest till he solves the riddle of his nightmares . . .

ZILLA GREEN
Whew! I . . . can feel it! Say. Why don't we go see if we can have a little talk with Floater?

BIRD NORTH
(distorts her face)
Whatever for? *You know,* a person's nuttiness rubs off after a while. *Well . . . okay.*

There is one tiny, red dot—way out on the moonlit sea.

ZILLA GREEN
(they both step forward onto the beach)
Sure. Let's go out on the Gulf and have a super conversation with Floater tonight. Awww . . . of all the luck. He's already floating, way out on the bay. I hope a giant barracuda doesn't get him!

BIRD NORTH
We just missed him? Now, that the guy knows how to "vacate." *Yep! You never know when you're going to see a barracuda!*

The two women leave the patio and arrive at the French doors in the lobby as they hear the splashing of water as several actors in cheesy, full-sized barracuda suits run up the aisles from the foyer and then out the side exits!

ZILLA GREEN

Wonder why Floater doesn't talk to anyone?

BIRD NORTH

A wise person once said, *"Those who judge don't matter. Those who matter, don't judge* — unless they've got an Absolute Truth worthy of rescuing an entire society."

ZILLA GREEN

Jesus — lady, let it also be mentioned that *"honesty — without compassion,* is just hostility!"

BIRD NORTH

Hey. I didn't want to put you on the defensive here . . . I wouldn't give you "a stone for bread, nor a snake for a fish."

ZILLA GREEN
(jokingly)

Defensive? *Nah!* But, has anyone told you you're so full of bologna that you could start your own delicatessen?

BIRD NORTH
(jokes back with a verbal coup
d'etat)
Has anyone ever told you that you're
so full of beans and that you cut-the-
cheese so often? You could sit down on
a slick-chair and play the seat-trumpet!

ZILLA GREEN
(chuckles)
No. No they haven't.

BIRD NORTH
(winks)
Well, now . . . they have.

ZILLA GREEN
You know, I really wish I could have
seen a barracuda!

REELY OLFF
(walks up and jumps in)
Ladies. *I think the Captain was right after
all!*

BIRD NORTH
Captain U.C. Bottom?! About what?

REELY OLFF
(butting into the conversation)
He said that when the "Security Inn"
(MORE)

BARRACUDA TALE

REELY OLFF (cont'd)
sign was accidentally reversed, it changed the luck of this motel just like it does with a ship.

ZILLA GREEN
(suddenly eats an oversized bologna sandwich from, seemingly, out of nowhere!)
I suppose? Anything's possible!

Parrot: "Wrak, Poly want a bologna sandwich!"

REELY OLFF
Yeah. And, that's when all the insecurity and those bad barracuda dreams began.

SANDBAG
(he narrates from the departing sailboat)
El Nino rains . . . washed the Florida beaches clean under torrential showers for the next few days, without stopping. Both up and down the coastline, there were serious property damage reports. However, Ft. Myers Beach made it through the storm with only its sign being torn down. Then the rain suddenly stopped and the sky cleared.

REELY OLFF
(sigh of relief)
Wow. That was quite a storm, Captain. Would you please make a damage-control report for me? And see if the guests are all right?

CAPTAIN U.C. BOTTOM
(with a new confidence)
Aye, Madam, I've already taken the liberty.
But I'm remiss to say that our good friend,
Floater, has drifted clear across the Gulf on
his red air mattress. Perhaps all the way to
Texas, by now! Galveston or Brownsville,
in the wind, I think.

REELY OLFF
(sad face)
Then what's happened to all our other
guests since the storm?

CAPTAIN U.C. BOTTOM
Don't you remember? Hey. That flying
coconut must have hit you pretty hard
on the head! You kicked Bird North
and Zilla Green out of this resort; just
before the big winds. So, they rented
a motor home and those gals went up
north for the rest of the winter.

REELY OLFF
And . . . Airbag? I mean, Sandbag?

CAPTAIN U.C. BOTTOM
Sandbag left about the same time — on
a pleasure yacht, with Doctor Indiahouse and his wife. He's gone to the
Keys as a hired sailing-hand, Madam.

BARRACUDA TALE

REELY OLFF
And, what about the parrot?

CAPTAIN U.C. BOTTOM
Oh, he flew the coop, too!

Parrot:"WRAK . . . GARGLE, WRAK!"

CAPTAIN U.C. BOTTOM
(dumbfounded)
Ahem, uh . . . I guess not!

REELY OLFF
(moans)
Any other problems?

CAPTAIN U.C. BOTTOM
The "Inn Security" sign fell down in the storm. But I have a proposition to make you, Madam Olff.

REELY OLFF
(stammers)
What-in-the world-is-it?!

CAPTAIN U.C. BOTTOM
As you know, the good Doctor India-house has kindly helped me face my nagging-fear of that recurring Barracuda Tale.

REELY OLFF
And . . . ?

CAPTAIN U.C. BOTTOM
It seems I'm not afraid of those pointy-toothed sea creatures after all!

REELY OLFF
Oh?! What are you afraid of, then, Captain?

CAPTAIN U.C. BOTTOM
H2O. Plain ol' water!

REELY OLFF
I knew it. I knew it! Your troubles have been a constant drip. Water-torture, I tell you!

CAPTAIN U.C. BOTTOM
(he sails)
But how could you have known?

REELY OLFF
Floater told me. He said you always avoided his wet, red rafts. His soaked air-mattresses!

CAPTAIN U.C. BOTTOM
I can accept that. So, with the insur-ance-money I received from my hur-
(MORE)

BARRACUDA TALE

CAPTAIN U.C. BOTTOM (cont'd)
ricane-battered vessel, I would like to
purchase this resort-motel and change
its luck with yet a new name.

REELY OLFF
(now returns to her usual mean-
ness)
Yes. You may buy it. But we'll talk
about it later.

CAPTAIN U.C. BOTTOM
No Madam. We'll talk about it now!

REELY OLFF
(she seethes)
What *did I just hear* you *say*?!

CAPTAIN U.C.BOTTOM
I said . . . there's going to be a few
changes made around here.

REELY OLFF
(smitten)
Such . . . as?

CAPTAIN U.C. BOTTOM
To begin with, you need to sell me this
resort and take a good vacation so you
can see the tropics for yourself.

REELY OLFF

Captain . . . I have to confess, I'm afraid of coconuts!

CAPTAIN U.C. BOTTOM
(comically-sympathetic punch-line)
I'm sorry. I didn't know you had the . . . "flying coco-phobia."

REELY OLFF
(dejected)
Of course you didn't know. Because Doctor Indiahouse had been working with me on it for an entire year. I'd sit under one palm tree a day. In the wind. Trusting that I was putting out my best anti-coconut vibes!

CAPTAIN U.C.BOTTOM
Again . . . my apologies, Madam.

REELY OLFF
(she now pries)
I know you're tired of your own fish-tales. But what are you actually going to call this resort motel—when you buy it from me?

Just then, FLOATER drifts by in the background, towing a new resort-motel sign into place. It's an extremely dumb-looking barracuda logo!

Suddenly, dozens of coconuts fall out of sky all around the actors.

(A slight pause . . .)

And then, a bucket of water hits them both in the face.

> CAPTAIN U.C. BOTTOM
> (now with a wistful and yearn-
> ing — punchline)
> I want to call this resort something straightforward and honest. Maybe something that a big fish could sink his teeth into! I know . . . I know. I'll call it: "The Aquaphobia by the Sea!!"

CLOSE CURTAIN

All of the actors walk onto the front stage beyond the curtain with laughable and oddball and phony-looking Velcro barracudas attached to their clothing. Then they bow with the sounds of ocean waves splashing about and water splashing on them.

THE END

POST SCRIPT

A coffee can of moonbeams

with oblivion in mothballs,

the claim of blessings

meant for the long-hauls.

A cup of street-wise,

with Serenity upon a string;

that's our circular-reasoning,

just swaying on a swing

BOOKS BY RORRY NIGHTTRAIN EAST

Passengers of Meandering Dream
The Night is a Panther
In the Gliding Sudden
August Messenger
Eventide Crows
The Ships Passing in the Desert
The Sixth Oath to The Winds
The Vacant City and Other Unusual Tales
Drastic Men of Clay
Runaway, Like a Dying Moon
Rob Tomb's Reality
A Tarantula's Dance in the Sun
Book in a Straitjacket
Barefoot Zeniths
Dents on A Fresno's Child
He Fell For Her .38's
Higher than a Shoulder's Ceiling
Forevermore and Lately
A Pocketful of Always
The Grist Mills of Unlimited Being
The Wafture of a Thousand Echoes
Immortal Tales of the Vampire's Dentist
The Sea Walker
The Soaring Never

BOOKS BY RORRY
NiGHT TRAiN EaST (CONT'D)

Vermilion Wayfarers to the Rain
Doors onto the Interior Realms
The Hands in a Jar of Stars
The Mind Control Clock
Walking a Haunted Sandbar
Once Upon a Polished Dystopia

◆

ABOUT THE AUTHOR

Rorry Nighttrain East a.k.a. R.L. Farr is truly a literary anomaly. At least, he's really not some kind of author to typecast, nor even place into any single mode or genre. For he seems to run all gamuts of poetry and prose, humor, short stories, screenplays, teleplays, and even novels. What's next from this versatile new talent?

He says he writes because he's handicapped; and we believe him: Laugh, cry . . . and then wipe the tears away. You've found yourself the pen pal of a lifetime. (With two artificial legs thrown in, to boot.) A repentant, imperfect Christian still under construction.

Born on July 18, 1952 in Fresno, California, he is an alumnus of De Anza College Cupertino, California and was formerly a journeyman automobile mechanic for a Lincoln Mercury dealership in San Jose, California.

He has since moved from the "Golden State" and now lives upon a sprawling ranch where he writes just outside the beautiful mile-high mountains of Silver City, New Mexico.

◈

RIVERSHORE BOOKS

www.rivershorebooks.com
blog.rivershorebooks.com
www.facebook.com/rivershore.books
www.twitter.com/rivershorebooks
Info@rivershorebooks.com

www.ingramcontent.com/pod-product-compliance
Lightning Source LLC
Chambersburg PA
CBHW070553030426
42337CB00016B/2475